HIEROGLYPH

A collection of Black poets

Ed Mabrey

Copyright ©2018 Ed Mabrey for Grumble Press LLC

All rights reserved. Published in the United States of America.

First Edition.

No part of this book may be reproduced or transmitted in any form, or by any means, electronic or mechanical, including photocopying, recording or by any information storage or retrieval system without permission from the publisher.

Layout and design: Ed Mabrey

Cover Art: Sean Mulkey

www.edmabrey.com

www.grumblepress.com

This book is dedicated to:

Taalam Acey, for the vision, heart and audacity to bring together very vital literary voices for his spoken word tour. The idea for creating something that would chronicle that gathering started with that tour and completes itself (for now) with this book.

All the members of that tour, including Taalam Acey, Lamar Hill, 13 of Nazareth, Jahiti of Brown FISH, Narubi Selah, Sunni Patterson, and myself.

Every person who purchased a ticket to those shows in every city and state we were in.

Every person that has supported each of us throughout the years.

Every person that picks up this book.

Every person that has ever went to a poetry event.

Table of Contents

Foreword	v
Star (a song) by Jahiti of Brown FISH	1
Black (for Will "Da Real One" Bell) by 13 of Nazareth	3
Forty Stories by Lamar Hill	8
Magic Trick Labyrinth by Taalam Acey	12
Ancestor Invocation by Sunni Patterson	16
Dizzy Answers the Journalists Question as to the Origin of BeBop by Ed Mabrey	18
Distant Lover by Lamar Hill	24
Cell-Block Celebrity by 13 of Nazareth	27
Oya by Sunni Patterson	33
Affirmation for Black Men by Taalam Acey	36
Science of Sport by Ed Mabrey	40
Strip 4 You by Lamar Hill	44
Shaken Not Scared by 13 of Nazareth	48
Be Good by Ed Mabrey	50
Willie Lynch LLC by Taalam Acey	53
Ancient Love-Poem by Sunni Patterson	57

Foreward

The Greek translation of the word means "sacred carving" and the original Egyptian definition leans more towards "the gods words".

This is where we find ourselves, at a crossroads of sorts between the two. Throughout history, the ability to write and read were considered a privilege reserved for the well bred, so to speak. Slaves of various nationalities weren't allowed to learn how to read or write, thus securing the classism and pecking order for generations to come.

Add to this the concept that letters and words as we have come to call them, are nothing more than glyphs, symbols which we, the writer and the reader, assign and give a certain amount of reverence and yes, power to. The ankh, the cross, the swastika, are all symbols. Yet at some point so were all 26 'letters' of the American/ English alphabet. Place these sacred carvings into a particular order, then have someone read them to the masses and, boom, you can affect the minds of countless individuals, because once the word moved from the written to the spoken it took on a life of its own.

While humans were talking to each other before they learned how to write and read symbols, something in us was changed once the word from our mouth was given a physical/visual form then read back to us. It, the word, became real, and in turn, so did we.

I liken this to how humans behaved prior to seeing their own reflection. How they lived changed drastically once one of them looked into a still pond, later as one realized it wasn't an enemy glaring at them but their own reflection in a piece of polished stone, then metals and eventually glass. They knew they existed and had shape, had form before seeing it, but having seen themselves they were a realized thing. A confirmation of 'I am a whole being' must have floated in their heads.

The ability to read and write was (and is still) used by many to speak as authority figures, serving as a go between from us to our religion, our god-source. How those religious books were translated, how those documents were formed, forged, and guarded, to be reviewed by a select few who were deemed worthy of translation, while the rest of humanity waited for a word from on high to know how best to please their god.

Each of the poets in this book have been lovingly referred to as 'gods'. In the modern Black community of poets and spoken word artists, it is considered a compliment of the highest order, a way of saying that the person being referred to is an architect and archetype, a person who was the original mold from which others voice or style has been cast from. Much like a nickname, it is not something one can bestow upon themselves, this title/compliment must be given.

So here we are, inside a book filled with symbols/glyphs, filled with sacred carvings of Gods words by Gods of The Word. The Spoken Word. Poems that were meant for the page and the stage, meant to break out of dusty halls and half forgotten shelves, poems meant to be heard and felt from the first row to the back of the room.

I was loathe to even use the typical Times New Roman for these poets words, then decided it was fitting to do so. As the Greeks and Romans translated or outright stole many things from African history, it suddenly seemed full circle to have a book of Black poets Black poems typed with a Papyrus font for Titles and Times New Roman font for some, most, or all of the poems. (as I type this I literally haven't decided if I will keep each in said font style or not, so this will be a revelation for us all, yes?)

The one constant I can promise is that the opening piece for the book are the lyrics to a song by one of the contributors. Be it church, a meeting, I felt most ceremonious events involving us Black folk often begin with a song, a prayer, libations, and then the good word follows. So the song is the first thing you'll encounter after this rambling of mine.

I can also promise the book will end with the only woman presence in the book. Why? Because in all things, balance. And all of creation (in my opinion) flows through women so it is only natural to close this book out with words from a Black woman.

I also promise the poems will not be sectioned together by author. I want you to sample each poet and jump from poet to poet. I am not saying there is any intentional thread between the poems, my only request to each poet was to share what they desired to share, and I can assure you they did not disappoint.

I cannot close this chat with you without mentioning the artwork for the cover. Sean Mulkey is one of the most vital visual artist of our time. When discussing what I wanted for the cover, I mentioned only two things to him; first, to think of Miles Davis *Bitches Brew* album and second, that the title of the book would be Hieroglyph. What he created is worthy of a book all to itself, the images, the symbolism, the detail, perhaps in the second run I will have him write a essay of everything that went into the creation of such a masterpiece.

Or maybe not. After all, he created a sacred carving to encapsulate the gods words. He did his part, I sincerely believe everyone in this book did theirs as well. I leave you to decipher these hieroglyphs as you will, and hope they inspire you to create carvings of your own.

I present to you- Jahiti of Brown FISH, 13 of Nazareth, Lamar Hill, Ed Mabrey, Taalam Acey, and Sunni Patterson.

Until that day,

Ed Mabrey

Founder,
Grumble Press LLC

Hieroglyph

...represents Africa's ancient language.

Jahiti of Brown FISH

Star (a song)
by Jahiti of Brown FISH

Don't go wishing on my star
'cause she's mine. She's the
daughter of the most high.

I realize from the space
and time of my mind,
realize I lied to my own
daughter's mind.

I committed a crime.

And, as long as you stay away,
shall my heart be penalized?
I can build a mountain but how
do I build a bridge of love to you?

I can paint a skyline but how do I
paint a perfect picture of me and you?
Don't go wishing on my star
'cause she's mine. She's the daughter
of the most high.

If I wasn't prepared, and I was a little
scared, lady let me know would you
still be there? Would you give me
time to prepare?

And, later on, when I reappear

Ed Mabrey

lady let me know would you still
be there?

I want to be everything you need.

So, lady, make sure exactly what you need.
Later on, when I'm on my knee and tears come
to your eyes, when you realize that this time
is your time, don't go wishing on my star
'cause she's mine.

She's the daughter of the most high.

Black (for Will "Da Real One" Bell)
by 13 of Nazareth

my photos are black
because I don't need titles
to define my relationships

my photos are black
because I don't require images
to remember my people

my photos are black
because the past two years
have been a period of mourning

my photos are black
because black absorbs the light
needed to dispel my dark shroud

my photos are black
because with all the light
I've absorbed I'm still searching
for the courage to say
"Let There Be…"

for the past 731 days
my frequency has been one
agonizing oscillation after the next

I walked around the same corner

Ed Mabrey

where Tupac saw Death and stared
directly into the faceless process

when I turned to walk away
Death started to breathe
down the back of my neck

in a high pressure cold stream
full of empty old dreams
the contact made
made my vertebrae freeze

been standing right here stiff
in the same spot ever since
the voice of A. Samson snatched
my Will to live through the phone
at 3 o'clock in the morning

in the mourning my will to live
began to die of the same wounds
left in the body of my brother
laying in a parking spot
familiar to the soles of my feet

I just stood there one week prior
laughing like we'd live forever
laughing like we did whenever

Miami became my home
for brief periods in time
in the Navigator
in both Chargers

Hieroglyph

on the passenger side
with my seat down low
window slightly cracked
and the beat down low
Biscayne Boulevard
blowing through my hair
Liberty City
looking me in the eyes
like freedom with amnesia

I never even bothered to remember
my way around Dade County
I was busy wearing Da Real One
like a blindfold entrusted with my life

a life protected so well
I mistook fragile for invincible
until my mind was fractured
into as many pieces
as Will and I had been places
as many pieces
as Will and I had held conversations
as many pieces
as Will and I had shared stages

poetry has not felt the same

I should not be leaving open mics
expecting the possibility of gunfire
I should not be thinking my features

Ed Mabrey

could be the gateway to my funeral
I should not be uncomfortable sitting
in houses of language I helped to build
I should not be listening to the artistic
endeavors of my colleagues and friends
as if I'm never going to hear them again

but I am
and I keep retracing every step
re-inhaling every breath
from the moment I got off the train
at approximately 6pm on May 21st
until the moment I got out the car
sometime after midnight on May 26th
in hopes of recalling something
anything I might have missed

but the only thing I miss
is the gentle giant
with the gold tooth smile
of a compassionate clown
who could conjure laughter
at the most inappropriate times

I could not be mad if he was around
I could not feel bad if he was around

I once had a seizure
in Fort Lauderdale
when I woke up
in the emergency room
at Holy Cross Memorial

Hieroglyph

Will was at my bedside
I smiled because I knew
he had to tell the hospital staff
he was my brother
in order to be where he was

I'll never forget his first words
"nigga, don't you die on me"
we laughed...
like we'd live forever

my photos are black
because forever came too soon

my photos are black
because forever came too soon

my photos are black
let there be light

Forty Stories
by Lamar Hill

Standing on the ledge, wondering if forty stories are enough to kill me.
Don't know if my woman would spit on my grave or be so overwhelmed
with grief that she'd just jump into the coffin with me.
Praying, Lord forgive me! For the forty souls that I've placed in a strangle hold,
trying to change a sentence of eternity in hell with no possibility for parole.

But it's forty stories straight down. Forty dead-end stories. Each one like a window
back through time. Each one harder to relate. Pictures of women whose bodies I've
treated delicately but whose hearts I've raped. Forty stories to the concrete where
I could finally get some sleep.

Forty stories dating back to when I was 13, in love with a beautiful brown beauty queen
with skin that smelled of cocoa butter, a voice like nothing I was used to and eyes so
deep I swore she could look into the future.

Wanting to apologize for my wandering eyes.
Wanting to apologize for the hard times.
Wanting to apologize for my low tolerance for temptation.

Hieroglyph

But instead, I'm forty love stories up just waiting, just praying. Forty stories up
with nothing but gravity between me and reality. Perhaps you've been here before.
Perhaps you have seen the world from this perspective. Perhaps you gazed down
on the unsuspecting? Perhaps you've even walked down the aisle only wishing
you could retrace your steps?

Perhaps you even believed in love, threw caution to the wind only to have your
heart broken and begin your trek up these forty stories again. Up here above it all,
feeling untouchable, feeling unlovable. Up here where the fear of being pushed is
so great you trust no one. You left your trust around the 25th floor 'cause it was
just too heavy for you to hold, and you left your ability to love unconditionally
around about the same place you left your soul.

So now you're up here alone with nothing but the baggage you refuse to release
the same baggage that prevents your peace. Forty stories leaving those that love
you safely down on the ground floor. So, no matter what the level of your financial
success, emotionally you will always be poor, and I'm just standing here my arms
spread wide, trying to find some kind of balance before I die.

Ed Mabrey

I keep hearing voices, although I try not to listen they have got me forty stories up
wondering if there is really something after this lonely existence. Wanting to do a
swan dive into the abyss, fearing I don't deserve to feel the softness of a true love's
kiss, fearing that happiness will always be just one floor out of my reach.

Just before I get ready to take the leap
                        SHE
                        SHE
                        SHE
Just across the way, the next building over
                    40 flights up with me
                        SHE
                        SHE
                        SHE
reaches for my hand and we take the leap together,
plummeting through the heartbreaks caused by others
that just made us stronger for each other.

Falling through the insecurity,
                falling through the doubt,
                      falling through past relationship hells,
Understanding that people don't change for people,

Hieroglyph

people change for themselves.
Falling through childhood crushes,
  finding love that is true,
    caught up in the hands of God when I
  finally
    conjure up the courage to say, I do.

Magic Trick Labyrinth
by Taalam Acey

I reside in the
Magic Trick Labyrinth,
where the average
is unacceptable
It need not be done,
or it best to be special.
Glory won't bless you.
Six billion souls will test.
Better think a dozen steps ahead,
or be hunted.

Be above par,
or completely
unwanted.

No one lusts energy
from the unextraordinary.
Either face fears,
or they'll be buried
along with your memory.

This realm is
pretend
or ascend.

Hieroglyph

What you scared of?
Demise behind every
corner you're unaware of.

Act like you need believers.
If God don't like ugly,
can you imagine how God feels
about underachievers?

Magic Trick Labyrinth

Come on child,
get your spells up.
Most epitaphs could read
Expected to be protected.

Doubt it or be 'bout it.
Whats'n'ever I do,
it's got to move
through corridors,
'cause boy, this world
will not only play you,
it will fillet you.

If your family could betray you,
what could six billion strangers do?

Ed Mabrey

Get your chops up,
or get chopped up.
They mop up.

Magic Trick Labyrinth

Even presidents, congressmen
and senators be minotaurs.
Lucidity is never stupidly achieved.
The stupid hardly ever achieve for long.

They be rich,
then they be flat broke,
then they be dead wrong.

Whatever you do, be feelin' it.
How you gon' play your cards
and not know what you dealin' with?
Intelligence could be irrelevant to the smart, quick.

Magic Trick Labyrinth

A million cats know
how to outrun you
by playing dumber.
You're thinking
you're mathematically

Hieroglyph

superior.
Them fools already
done had your number.

Had you on speed dial
and in their top five
since birth. Wake up,
learn your worth.

They eat their young here!
Wasn't just a hundred years
of lynching. The unsuspecting
will always get hung here.

Get your paranoia up,
or get your panorama shut.
At the end of the day guess what?
It's the end of the day.

Take your life for a joke
and half the folk at your funeral
will be holding back laughter.

Magic Trick Labyrinth

And just like the game of death,
the next level of difficulty
comes after.

Ancestor Invocation
by Sunni Patterson

Ancestor
Breath
Bridge

Carry us
                    over
              tumultuous time

You
              who can hear
              and answer with
                quick remedy

Ready
              before we ask
                  You
              who can speak
           through tongues of
          trees & fire & water

Earth cannot hold you
              We pound the ground
                You appear

Oh, Ancient Ones
            You who can make
              lightning strike
          with the flick of a skirt

Hieroglyph

You who can make
>> tornado turn with
>> the spin & span of hips

Take us there
>> To the place of knowing
>> The hall that leads to the doorway of
>> You

Oh, Holy Ones
>> You of the first light
>> You who know the
>> potential of possibility
>> pulsing in the dark

Deliver us unto our gifts
>> You who have sunlight
>> in your fingertips

Touch our drums
>> Make us hear the rising
>> Make us move

A steady stomp

Dizzy Answers the Journalists Question as to the Origin of BeBop
by Ed Mabrey

Dizzy: "Every year I play it gets harder to play this thing."
Interviewer: "Really I thought after all these years it'd be easy for you."
Dizzy: "Not at all, you could live to be a thousand years old and never master this thing.
But it also gets harder to put it down. It calls to me you see. I know it's in there
sitting in the case smiling, waiting to see what I think it's going to teach it,
excited to think about how it's going to humble me."

Be bop
African blues
Anti swing
Un swing
Big bang quasi bang
Cheraw South Carolina
Music class tried to give me a trombone
All that was left in the class but my little arms
could only reach 4th position
That's like a ferarri staying in 1st gear
Can't v r o o m
Can't vroom
Next door neighbor heard a blocked engine
Let me borrow his trumpet now and then

Hieroglyph

Man look
Music all around you
Don't have to be a genius like me to get it
Met the wife at Howard theater
in Washington DC 1938
Locked that down in '40
Best song I never finished
Hope she dance to the end
after I play my last note

Look here it is
Column of stone paint from brush
Idea of man mind made real in oil
Call to the oil to the ink to the alabaster
Closer to this than the flesh

Look here it is
I seen 8 presidents come and go
Been in the White House more than them
Favorite? Peanut farmer Jimmy Carter
Salted peanuts play from Georgia gas stops boiling
Cut Calloway's butt with a knife for lying on me
Ain't nothing to it just trimming the fat

Look here it is
Bird flew the cuckoo nest but never got high in front of me
Monk fixed racism by playing between the notes
Blakely, Shorter, Hawkins, Chuy, Guy, Felipe,
Names sound like God bless you, gesundheit, and amen

Ed Mabrey

Miles always searching for tomorrow like some soap opera
that has become self-aware of its shelf life
Trane fighting the good fight, always in a war with some god
or some devil for our souls all our souls humanities souls on ice

Cleaver and the Panthers and the Liberated Front reminding us
that in addition to knees to kneel we also were born with legs to stand
and fists to fight

Malcolm and Ossie
Our precious black rosary beads we click and hum
Rotate them in hand while making dow or praying in a juke joint at sunset
Laying down placemats and asking someone to point us in the direction of east
East man east
Never heard of east?
To the east my brother to the east my brother to the east?
Are you on point Tip, all the time Phife?
This is protected by the Red the Black and the Green with a key?
My posse down on Broadway?
It's like a jungle sometimes it make me wonder how I keep from going under?
White lines? If you gonna ride ride the white horse?
No sleep till Brooklyn?
Is Brooklyn in the house?
Who stole my Harlem?

Hieroglyph

Chicago on fire, Redhook burning Matty Rich?
Illadelph halflife?
And that's the double truth, Ruth!
You know, east?

Look man here it is
Lee Roi went all Baraka on y'all but you wasn't listening
Page 47 of his magnum opus *Transbluency*
Parker told y'all
My wife say it every morning after cooking eggs
Roots said *it's in the music turn it up let it rock*
Let it rain on the block till the neighbors call the cops
The cops gone come but they ain't gone do ish
They don't want no problem what are y'all stupid
It's all in the music it's all in the music

See right there
You was too scared to hear it
Keep thinking God gonna come down
with doves and cookies and milk
and stroke your face softly, hand you
a vip card and take you to the back of the club
I met God
Yesterday, last Thursday, this morning
God sleeps in that there trumpet case
Wakes me up every morning
I keep thinking I'll show her what I've learned
She smiles a silver O against my lips
And thinks on how she'll humble me today
We didn't name it bebop
Some dumb reporter did
But he was smart enough to hear it

Ed Mabrey

God talking, he just couldn't make out
what she was saying
So when you ask me what be bop is,
that's what it is, God talking in modern jazz
and only allowing us to hear the final two sounds
as words to our ears
They sound like be bop
Listen

HIEROGLYPH

The literal translation of the word hieroglyph is "sacred symbol," but thinking of the term invokes an idea of images which contain meanings in addition to those most obviously indicated. Meanings which require knowledge not overtly related to the images themselves.
-13 of Nazareth

Distant Lover
by Lamar Hill

Distant lover, you've been gone so long
that if I had the ability to turn myself into a bolt
of electricity, I would fly through the phone.
I'd be by your side before you could put your
tee-shirt and panties on.

Distant lover,
I sit here on the line recalling the way I
stuttered the first time your eyes met mine,
how your legs felt around my waist,
the sweet way your insides taste,
how I seemed to speak in tongues when I
moved inside your space.

Distant lover, please come back home.
I'll beg if I have to, this time around
I'll try harder to understand. I realize
love stings, and these stings have me
in the jewelry store sizing rings.

Distant lover, please come back to me.
I know my boys were a problem before,
but from now on when I see them through the
peephole I won't even answer the door.

I apologize for the lying. I'm tired of waking
up with a dick hard enough to cut diamonds.
I know I didn't always comment when you

Hieroglyph

wore something sexy to bed, or did something
new with your head.

But now, at two in the morn when I hear our song,
I find myself running to the phone so that you
can describe to me what you have on. And I know
in the past you questioned my fidelity, but distant lover
I swear I'll cut it off before I put it inside of another.

Distant lover, if you return to this covenant
I'll wear a sign on my back saying,
Pussy-whipped, AND LOVING IT!

I realize that truth flows from the mouths of
babes, but I swear I could never tell a lie when I was
between your legs.

What in God's good name was I thinking about
when I let you slip away? The way you stole food
off my plate or sips from my drink? Right now,
I'm so lonely I'd even settle for you bitching
about me leaving dishes in the sink.

Distant lover, I'm dying a slow death.
Life without you ain't nothing but stress.
I'll hold the phone to my heart, so you can
hear it beating in my chest. I know in the past
I took more than I gave, but distant lover,
if you come home, I will pack a lunch and
go down on you all day.

Distant lover what more can I do,

Ed Mabrey

what more can I say? Fuck this phone,
you stay where you are,
I'm on my way.

Cell-Block Celebrity
by 13 of Nazareth

I had a whole lot to say
I decided against it

thought it was a man's world
'til I studied the women

wanted a life of fame
but I visited prison
and found both to be the same
celebrated different names

just numbers
                                  rap song
                                  rap sheet
either way behind bars
                            just one got beats
the other got beef

shanks to the abdomen
award winning speech

thanks to the audience
respect on the street

a credibility gauge
if the hood don't agree

fuck what whoever say
if the hood don't love 'em

Ed Mabrey

them niggas can get the grave
                if the hood's disrespected
                    retaliate right away

these attitudes put my people in a cage
same attitude put my people on a stage

funny thing is
all of 'em got chains

some iron
some gold
sum prison
sum fame

I guess the value of the metal
is the value of the man

in the eyes of society
I wonder what's the plan

I wonder if the ignorance
                that sends us to the slammer
is the same type of ignorance
                that turns us into fans

like being on television
makes you more than a man

like being sent to prison
makes you much less than

Hieroglyph

the average person is a victim of propaganda
even the term 'average person' is propaganda

in this campaign for the slaves and masters
see the paradigm don't shift
                if the people don't assist
                and the people don't assist

if the people don't know what a paradigm is
or how the system of practice affects them
            on a day to day basis

textbooks mean nothing if you strugglin' for basic
food
clothing
shelter
dependable transportation

traveling in a circle to all the same places
social lines drawn keep people in their places

in this Kentucky Derby you're a horse
                keep racin'
did you borrow yo ass from a horse?!
                keep shakin'

I apologize
I think you're amazing

but if I don't objectify you
the radio won't play it

Ed Mabrey

and if the radio don't play it
the people who need it most
will never hear what I'm sayin'

sacrifice duly noted
you're a goddess and I know it

from the blasphemy and veneration
of every lyric spoken

see this whole industry is devoted
to the woman's body

we bless it then we curse it
we love it then we hurt it

we speak of all its value then
we treat it like it's worthless

yet regardless of position
women figure ways to work it

to empower themselves
making heaven outta hell

she's only naked due to faith
in men saying sex sells

so she spreadsheet vagina
micro soft excel

Hieroglyph

make it clap like a round of applause
                                    hell yeah
and if you wonder why
I'm coming with thunder around here
                            I brought peace
you told me to be a saint elsewhere

HIEROGLYPH

I spoke Hieroglyphs in English class
picture worth 1000 words
I wrote an eye full
my dissertation was longer than the bible
Lamar Hill

Oya
by Sunni Patterson

Wild women
                walk with buffalo
             have lightning on their tongues
                flywhisks as weapons

Wild women
                walk with machetes
                walk with wisdom
                with grace and ease

Wild women
              have hurricanes in their bellies
              release a flood of a lesson

Wild women   fly free
              watch their ways
              how   they rip
              and shred

Who can understand her

A winding Niger River of a woman
            who is unafraid to tear away
         to roam then become the wind

She who speaks in gusts and cyclones
            blasts us back to high ground
            high consciousness

Ed Mabrey

She turns and so does the world

Feel her spin
                spanning several lifetimes

Hear her speak
                sparking alarm

See her dance
                summoning the dead

Resurrect new life

Heaven hears her
                knock on the door

She safely transports the ones
who call for her assistance

Wild women
                open portals to new worlds
                    new speech
                    new dreams

Oh, dearly beloveds
so dearly departed
from the ways of the guardian

Beware

Wild women

Hieroglyph

are not to be tamed
only admired

Just let her in
and witness her set your days ablaze

Affirmation for Black Men by Taalam Acey

I am young, gifted and black.
In any environment I will adapt.
If you throw me in an office,
I will Access my PowerPoint to Excel.Word.

My Outlook ain't 'bout being shook.
They done put me in jail cells.
When it comes to hell,
I take it like I give it.

When it comes to life
I often live it like I'm livid.
Ain't on no DL. I'm on my DHL,
where every message gets delivered.

Shit's serious. Grown man got no time
for the delusional or the delirious.
Came to live a memorable life,
die an honorable death,

in between do what I can
to make the best of this experience.
Productive, not counter. Not self-
destructive. I be about balance.

Some people be about frontin'
And some people be about violatin'.
That's why I try to be about patience
till it's got to be about violence.

Hieroglyph

Talent and incredible focus internal
locus of control. Good thing this earth
suit is somewhat attractive because most
cats would be taken aback

if I had to bare my soul. It's beautiful
and it's grizzly. Please excuse me if
I don't fuck around. Life ain't playing
and yet it's a game. And I got a few seeds

with a stake in my name. And, by the time
they have seeds, there needs to be no mistakin'
my name. And I love my blood sweat and tears.
Lacing up my boots tight and outpacing my pain.

I am young, gifted and black, I will adapt
wherever you throw me at. My demographic
means I have to be versatile. Work an ice grill
and still be able to work a smile.

Being 100% hood is virtually worthless now,
besides, there's too many rings up in this circus
now. So, whether it's that juke joint jumpin' or
that corporate function, you can put me in a workshop
all day,

or throw a black and a 40 in my hand
and put me in a project hallway. Then, afterwards,
interview all the executives and all the dope boys

Ed Mabrey

and I guarantee you they all say that

wherever I choose to fit in, I will lay like wallpaper.
Air tight, body healthy, head right. Stretch'em both
out every night. When I fall down, I begin again.
I be my own life coach like,

"Mu'fucker you better win in the end." Fake friends
I brush off. Failures I dust off and evolve. When I'm
afoot in my yard, I build fences. Cats wanna act
like they measure up to rulers, but they ain't even half
inches.

When I look to my God, I begin with,
"I promise to change problems into opportunities
until you see fit that my life is ended."

I am young, gifted and black and I will adapt
to whatever it takes. Available time determines
available breaks, so when there's no time there's
no restin'. Just like when you show no grind

you get shown no blessings. And God made me gifted
so how can I not personify presence? My essence is
earth,
wind, fire, water and ether. Be the medium darkness or
light,
my light still permeates through either.

I'ma be the best me that I can. Anything that tests me
I plan to aggressively withstand. Any soul that tries to

Hieroglyph

oppress me be damned. I am young, gifted and black
and I will adapt till my spirit is free.

And, till they execute my will,
my will-will execute my world.
Anything and everything I choose,
it shall be.

Science of Sport
by Ed Mabrey

"Float like a butterfly sting like a bee
Your hands can't hit what your eyes can't see"

(There are several steps from star to supernova)

I was born of a painter, is it any wonder I'm an artist? Fists for brushes, lips drip Louisville red dirt drops sweat in summer sun, red like my stolen bike. Last time anyone take my speed from me. My ability to fly. Left hand named Preakness. Right Kentucky derby. Let me knock the blue off your face, onto white canvas square, blood Jackson Pollocked pretty like the only flag I'll ever salute.

(Tremor symptoms occur on one side of body only)

The year I was born the first rocket crossed into outer space.

(When a massive star exhausts its fuel it explodes as a supernova)

First time I felt God was when I came back with a gold medal round my neck. Didn't know something so small could be so dense, hold so much weight. *Wait you can't sit here, nigger entrance round back* roundhouses me. I whirlwind

Hieroglyph

medal into the Ohio River. Watch it turn the water red, then black, then green.

> (In stage two of Parkinson's walking problems and poor posture might become apparent)

1964- the name Cassius Clay begins messing up my boxing, too much coon in my uppercut,
jigga boo in my jab, right away suh in my right hook. So I leave those slave letters in Sonny Liston's limp corner. Exit the ropes Muhammad Ali.

> (The outer parts of the star are expelled violently into space while the core collapses under its own weight)

> (Stage three- loss of balance and slowness of movement significantly impair activities of daily living such as dressing and eating)

In 1967 I said, *"I ain't got no quarrel with them Viet Cong, Viet Cong ain't ever called me nigger."*

Uncle Sam greased his gloves with racism, smeared it on my eyes while we were clinched in the corner. All I could see was no food for my family, hands tied behind my back, gloves covered in space dust and government supplied opium wars. Say if you won't kill men for us we won't let you beat them up. Say quasi logic, say make love not war, say Sputnik, say Tricky Dick, say only the

Ed Mabrey

penitent shall pass, say 2nd amendment never accounted for assault rifles, say Mickey Mouse got blood on his hands.

1971- First impact into Mars. Joe Frazier sends me into orbit. I take the time to find east, break bread with Allah.

> (Stage four of Parkinson's- movement requires a walker and person is unable to live alone)

Lie down with me George. Before I smack you into selling Foreman grills, let me show you this ain't no boxing ring; it's a bed, corner posts be mattress, canvas be box spring, rope-a-dope be a pillow. Sleep now you beautiful giant, wake up a healed man. Let this hook knock the demons out of you. Too much Don King in your blood, German Sheppard in your bite.

Listen to my lullaby George.
Ali bumaye Ali bumaye

1975- the first orbit around Venus. It took the Thrilla in Manilla for me and Frazier to realize we were in love with each other. He didn't quit in the ring. Anything that Black and beautiful don't know quit. No, Joe saw the truth in me, us two planets, he all Earth and me all Venus. I broke his heart, not his spirit. He's the closest thing to a brother I ever had; my melanin Jesus.

Hieroglyph

"I am America, I am the part you won't recognize, but get used to me. Black, confident, cocky, my name not yours, my religion, not yours, my goals, my own. Get used to me."

(No known repulsive force can push back hard enough to prevent gravity from collapsing the core into a black hole)

(The final stage of Parkinson's-)

Look man, shut up. Told y'all years ago, wasn't no Parkinson's, ain't you been listening?
I'm the way and the light, boxing was just a way to get you to pay attention to my message, love.
Just love. I've been holding in this love and light till I thought y'all could handle it. Till I felt you needed it most. These ain't Olympic torch tremors, this is what a star looks like before it goes black hole. These shakes are supernova. Remember, Float like a butterfly, sting like a bee.
Their guns can't hit what their bigotry can't see. Rumble young man, rumble young lady, rumble. The champ is here. The champ is here.

Strip 4 You
by Lamar Hill

She said she wanted to make love with strings
attached, but only to her arms and wrists
Said she had her heart broken too many times
to ever consider going through it again

Said she only wanted the physical
She said she wanted me to fill her chest
with my treasure
then afterwards forget I had ever even met her

But there was something about the way her
insides tasted, after they had marinated over
night, that made me wonder what it would take
to make this woman wake up next to me
for the rest of my life

To abandon my feelings of abandonment
To make every woman before her a blur
See the fact of the matter is I want to reinvent the
wheel with her

I want to find different reasons to fall in love
every single minute
That's why I contemplate different positions
to keep her interested
each and every time that I'm in it

That's why I treat her sweat like holy water
trying to absorb every drop into my skin

Hieroglyph

So, when I'm going through the rigmarole of my
day I can always revert back to her skin

So, I told her to strip for me
I told her to take off that thing that makes it
impossible to commit
and commit to getting rid of it

Told her to take off the stigma
of failed relationships in the past
Told her to forget about her ex-man
Told her to take off all the baggage
and just stand here in front of me naked

Told her sex was cool but making love is sacred
Told her to forget about the past dude's behavior
Forget how he disrespected you in front of your
girlfriends and neighbors

Forget all the nights when the only number you
had for him was a pager
Forget how you stayed up losing years off your
life

Wondering if he was even gonna bother
to come home tonight
Forget about the bumps and the bruises
the lies and excuses

Forget about the mediocre lovemaking
that he didn't even bother to shower for
Because in my eyes you're a virgin

Ed Mabrey

as pure as the blackest night

Sure, you've given your body away
a few times
but you've never bothered to open up your mind

In the same way the moon
has power over the sea
you have power over me

I won't be satisfied until you come
nine times
Why nine?
Because nine is the number of completion

It serves notice to the Creator that we have
found peace within
But first I want you to strip for me

Take off the memories
of every ill-fated one-night stand
Every failed second chance
All the nights you stayed up wanting romance

Take off all the years of misery
Feeling like you had to endure his bullshit
cause y'all had history
I want you to unbutton the suffering
I want you to unzip the unhappiness
I want you to slide out of the doubt
cause it's all about you

Hieroglyph

Every time I step into the room
I'm consumed by the power
that exudes from your womb

He was a fool
not to pay homage
to a goddess
Your body is timeless

I want you to strip for me
Soul bare
Spirit open
Mind focused

Believe you deserve love just like the rest
Believe your body can be used for more than sex
I want you to strip for me
Emotionally

Then I want us to start new
I want you to strip for me
cause I've already
stripped for you

Shaken Not Scared
by 13 of Nazareth

I am a trip to the hospital waiting to happen
I am the shattering of my loved ones' nerves
I am consciousness with temporary amnesia
I am flying down a flight of stairs face first

I am conversation without recall
I am biting my tongue until it bleeds
I am the lost control of motor skills
I am piss in a new pair of jeans

I am chaos without warning
I am the alteration of previous plans
I am laying helpless in a crosswalk
I am the reason for unusual traffic jams

I am dependent upon the kindness of strangers
I am falling at your feet all the time
I am a soft heart trapped in a hard place
I am vulnerability personified

I am always struggling to figure out why
I am here in the last place I ever dreamed
I am staring death in the absence of a face
I am a crumbling bridge over a troubled stream

I am crashing into the fire hydrant at the corner
I am limp body against airbag and car door
I am crashing into the walls of crowded venues

Hieroglyph

I am limp body against a hotel lobby floor

I am oxygen mask and intravenous fluids
I am fractured bones and sutured flesh
I am sharp pains and missing time
I am involuntary movements and dripping sweat

I am an earthquake with self-awareness
I am a tornado with arms and legs
I am twenty years living with epilepsy
I am shaking but I am not scared

Be Good
by Ed Mabrey

I cried for you today,
moved a mountain,
made water from wine,
took the salt from my tears
to melt the snow in your eyes.

I cut my locs and buried a handful
in your front yard, gave God my
two week notice, sent rsvps to my
demons.

Told the skeletons in my closet
to wear something pretty and purple
for your arrival, smacked the brightness
out of the sun, sucked the blue from the sky
and buried it in your name, stole the black keys
from your piano. I cried for you today.

What else would you like for me to do?

I walked under a ladder 13 times
while holding a black cat. I sprinkled broken
mirrors on your path like rose petals, spilled salt
on the table called it luck, burned my rabbits foot,
called it destiny, challenged the wind to a breath holding
contest.

Told old lady tarot to give me your death

Hieroglyph

card to swallow, changed my name to whatever
is on your mind right now, changed yours to thank you
may I have another, thank you may I have another, thank you
may I have another.

Beat yesterday until it apologized.
Will you love me now? Love me like wings love breeze,
like a whip splitting air, just one kiss is all I ask, with a tongue
that tastes like tomorrow and lips made of forever.

I listened to the bearded man, I trimmed my lion claws,
I cut my mane. Pull my tail, lie me on your table, sacrifice me.
Cut me till I split your rock. I don't want your wardrobe.
The witches sweets don't tempt me, I'm your lion.

You can have my roar. Coward me into submission,
dance around these ribs, take the tired muscle resting within,
eat of my flesh, strip me and make me whole. Make an arrow
of my heart, shoot it at the moon. Tether it to everything I've said.
I'll pull it down for you.

Place midnight in your hand and my name in the other.
Clap me into oblivion, razor me with your laughter.
I cried for you today. Tell me it makes sense.

Ed Mabrey

Tell me pain is pleasure and punch me orgasm.
Tell me down is up and elevate me hell.
Take the t from my tears and make me ear you.
Take the f from my fears and make me ear you.
Take the h from my here and make me ere you.

I will wait like a slave waits for freedom that never comes.

How do I love thee let me haiku the ways-
I cried for you today
I cried for you today
I cried for you too

Be whatever you want,
just be home when I get there.
Go wherever you wish,
just be my everywhere.
I don't care that you've got me.
Crack my ribs with the key hidden
beneath your tongue.
Place me inside your cage,
dance inside my secret places.
Let me pace inside the walls of your hopes
and I will hum you eternity.

Willie Lynch LLC
by Taalam Acey

In these times of poor,
somewhat righteous poets
and completely co-opted
Manchurian emcees,
where your favorite poet
is probably all too familiar with
Top Ramen
and your favorite rapper's owner
still obligates him
to get back on his knees
shit be happening.

And when poets act like rock stars,
we call those false prophets.
And when rappers act like
they getting far more money
than they are,
we call those false profits.

And Willie Lynch LLC
needs MC's
who can be MD'd
by BG's.

So, if you want to see G's,
they willing to put you out,
long as you willing to let them
turn you out. Be 'bout that time-tested

Ed Mabrey

"destroy-our-youth" focus group
propagandized company message.

Dear children,
the key to your success
is in doing anything you can think of
that might possibly get you arrested.

Ain't 'bout hard work.
No.
Stay high.
Stay drunk.
Be disrespectful.
Assault people.
Tote weapons.

Family, Willie Lynch LLC
has mastered the essence of
making sure most will never be
everything they can be.
They attack the weak.
Tell 'em, "There's this savage inside
you called a nigga' and it's just dying to be free".

Then Willie tells its cadre of contracted emcees
that they are bound by service level agreements.
Make sure they find ways, per song,
to say, "Free your inner nigga!" at least 25 times.
And every time you say it, say it differently
to correspond to some punch lines and rhymes.

And it's like Willie read minds

Hieroglyph

'cause if you're a potential sell-out
Willie know how to find out.

First, he rub your back with that warm contract.
Then, he tickle your chin with that pen
Then, when he slide that rider deep inside ya,
if he hear you moan, he know he got you configured
to murder some innocent children,
like remote controlled pilot and military drones.

And Willie got ample sambos over samples.
They use damn fools as examples
to confuse self-respect and dismantle pride.

So, if a decade of negativity
helps influence a young woman
to be a gold-digger
and helps influence a young man
to be a criminal,
that's just a result of
those Willie emcees doing their job
for the many wealthy people
who would love to see you dead,
who know how to use a proxy
to identify and popularize Uncle Toms.

Who would gladly
serve them
your head
on a platter
for little more

Ed Mabrey

than crumbs on a table.

So, the next time you hear a rapper
spitting some ignorance that,
based on your understanding
of the way things work,
don't make no damn sense,
there's a perfectly rational explanation sir.
That mother-fucking rapful abomination
must work for Willie Lynch LLC.

Ancient Love-Poem
by Sunni Patterson

Where do I begin?
Shall I count the ways?
Shall I count the amount
of sunrises and sunsets,
count the days,
the nights,
the time?

Let me honor you without a limit.
If this were just physical
time would play
a much bigger part
but, dear heart,
we are much more
ancient than that.

Sanskrit sacred,
full moon flavored,
the power of creation
fills this space.
Fuse ourselves one.
Each move, a tune,
each tune, a tool.

This is the true art of alchemy,
the holiest matrimony,
most mystical marriage,
a mantra of magic

Ed Mabrey

ascended masters
like craftsmen,
your life like my ladder.

Push me higher,
make me taller,
no catching if I fall
knowing I'm falling
on love
or in light.

Pure joy,
unbridled bliss,
this is walking on wind,
a pilgrimage past
our former selves
into the future of a new return.

Ancestors rejoice,
angels applaud
cosmically calling us home,
and here we are;
present,
perfect
on purpose.

A continuous stream of prayer
all in praise of the sacred,
where lovemaking
is equivalent to meditation.

Hieroglyph

This is not for the uninitiated,
only those willing to go
through the transformation
      for a time
we are formless,
feather-like light,
there is no end to us.
      We are much more ancient than that.

Crossroads
by Sunni Patterson

there is a place
where head   meets heart
                                     meets world
                        meets every point in between

the line where sky
                                  meets water
                                  meets earth
                                  meets flame

oh,
                              wayfaring wanderer
sojourner
                              of truths
caution on the road

for One is always watching
                     with cowrie colored eyes
wide   with child-like wonder
                     innocent and ancient

secular secrets
sacred medicine
manifested matter
connects us one to another
while we are here
                              in the middle
                              of the way

Hieroglyph

at the entrance of the gate

pleading
do not confuse me
in this world
of possibilities
of choice
of chance
of intuition
of logic
of knowing
of prayer
where 3 become 1
where past
                              meets present
                              meets future
where seed
                              meets soil
                              meets plant
where One
                              is always watching
guiding us
                              to enlightenment
mediating our existence
while we resolve
within ourselves
                              our heavens
                              our hells
                              our hiddens
                              our seens
and every point in between
all while being here

Ed Mabrey

in the middle of the way

Jahiti is a singer/songwriter based in the United States. As part of Baltimore's legendary group, Brown FISH, he has performed throughout the US, Canada and Jamaica for the past 18 years. Bringing his own brand called World, Country, Reggae, Soul, Jahiti continues to build his solo legacy while remaining close to the spirit of the Brown FISH name since the untimely death of his best friend and musical partner Derrick "OOH" Jones.

As an artist, Jahiti isn't just about the music. A former educator, community organizer and youth advocate, Jahiti has dedicated himself to the Baltimore community and continues to share his talents and passion in and with other communities that reflect similar challenges.

Whether it's marching in the streets to end domestic violence, reading and singing to a 1st grade class or performing in the prisons, he is committed to using his celebrity and talent to make a difference in the world.

With a musical style described as a mix between Johnny Cash, Bob Marley, Richie Havens and Bob Dylan we encourage you to find out for yourself.

Ed Mabrey

Visit jahitiworld.com to learn more about the artist and his work.

Since making the decision to dedicate his life to his art, 13 of Nazareth has published 8 CD's, been touring throughout the United States, Canada, the United Kingdom, co-founded a publishing company and a poetry awards ceremony, earned several regional and national slam titles, and been featured on television and radio. The golden thread which runs throughout his hip-hop infused poetry is drawn from the looms of various spiritual traditions to weave a tapestry of creative works geared toward the personal and collective healing process.

13 of Nazareth is a convergence of Hip-Hop culture, old school R&B/Soul music, scientific spirituality and a child-like love of language. Rhythms that are warm to the heart embedded with lyrics that are challenging to the ear often emerge from this intersection and have resulted in him being labeled a "poet's poet." His writing is elevated without being condescending as it invites seeing from his vantage point without dismissing that of others. 13 of Nazareth encourages each listener/reader to apply what is useful from his work while discarding what is not.

Ed Mabrey

For more info go to www.13ofnazareth.net

Born March 6, 1974, in Newark, New Jersey to Constance McCloud and George Hill, Lamar Anthony Hill is without question one of the greatest pure writers of his generation. Lamar has countless poems to his credit and is perhaps best known for his spoken word, but poetry does not even scratch the surface of what this man has accomplished. The fact of the matter is Lamar does not even consider himself a poet first. If you were to ask him, he would tell you first and foremost, he is a playwright, with five plays under his belt, all of which have been performed for sold out crowds and standing ovations. Secondly, he considers himself a novelist who has written three books, all of which have been heaped with praise. Lastly, he will tell you about the countless poems he has written, the eight poetry CDs that have sold hundreds of thousands of copies all over the world, and the huge numbers of people that have been affected by his work.

Ed Mabrey

Lamar is a graduate of the University of South Carolina, in Orangeburg South Carolina, where he majored in business and minored in Theatre. He is also a graduate of the oldest performing arts high school in the country, the esteemed Arts High School in Newark, New Jersey, where he majored in acting.

If you have ever had the privilege of seeing Mr. Hill perform, you know he is a whirlwind of energy with the ability to take the audience on a rollercoaster ride of emotion. Whether speaking on the spiritual, political, or his special brand of relationship poetry, few are able to capture the attention of an audience the way he does. No one questions that Mr. Hill is special and he, in his own words, hasn't even begun to show the world all of what he is truly capable.

For more info go to facebook.com/lamaranthonyhill

Ed Mabrey is a poet, comedian, actor/voice actor and motivational speaker. He's been on TVOne, HBO, Crackle, NBC, CSPAN, CNN, ABC, FOX, Congo Network.

Ed's work has been commissioned by the National Civil Rights Museum for the MLK50 Commemoration and the 2017 Freedom Awards.

Ed is the only 4-time Individual World Poetry Slam Champion. Featured 3 times on Lexus' Verses and Flow (TVOne). Ed has been on every season of AllDef Digital.

You've seen him on Button Poetry and WAN Poetry. He is a 3-time Southern Fried Regional Individual Poetry Slam Champion. The winningest (yep we made a word for him) poet in Slam History, Ed Mabrey has been touring professionally and has performed at over a hundred colleges and universities, delivered TedX talks (2015/2017), shared stages with everyone from Saul Williams, Buddy Wakefield, Andrea Gibson, The Roots, Gil Scott Heron, The Last Poets, Amiri Baraka, Jill Scott, Ursula Rucker, Eric Robeson, Dwele, Middle Child, Raheem DeVaughn, Mary Mary, Jazmine Sullivan, Denzel Washington and many more.

For info and booking go to edmabrey.com or edmabrey@gmail.com

"You have so, so much inspired me with your Spoken Word" said the legendary Stevie Wonder, while interviewing Taalam Acey, during Wonder's own birthday celebration in May 2008. Taalam, a child of the Newark Rebellion, was raised by a single mother who was a member of the famed writer and activist Amiri Baraka's community organization. Acey is an independent artist whose work has been featured frequently on TV One and was selected as the original "number one thing you need to know about" on BET's countdown show, "The 5ive." Over the years, BET has featured and aired roughly half-a-dozen segments featuring Taalam Acey. The Newark, NJ native's poetry has appeared in Essence Magazine and Susan Taylor, the magazine's Editor Emeritus, personally invited Acey to perform for an audience of six thousand at The Essence Music Festival in New Orleans. Acey was selected as the initial presenter for the inaugural Baltimore

TEDx. He was also the curator of the 2011 Sacred Circle Cafe at New Jersey's most prestigious theater, the NJ Performing Arts Center. Taalam was honored to be a guest of Congresswoman Maxine Waters for the Congressional Black Caucus' 2007 & 2008 "Young Gifted and Black" panels. He has shared his work in several countries and approximately one hundred schools of higher education; including the esteemed Graduate School of Education at UC Berkeley, where he delivered a lecture on contemporary Spoken Word. Taalam Acey has recorded more than a dozen CDs and authored four books.

Additionally, films that include his work have garnered an Audience Award (2002) and a Special Jury Prize (2006) at the Sundance Film Festival. He was featured in an acclaimed Radio-One London slam poetry documentary and Marc Smith, the founder of slam poetry, used Acey's work in his definitive book.

To learn more go to www.taalamacey.com

Originally from New Orleans, Louisiana, Sunni Patterson combines the heritage, culture, and traditions of her native town with a spiritual worldview to create powerful music and poetry.

Emerging from the musical womb that is New Orleans, Sunni Patterson combines the heritage of her native town with an enlightened modern style to create music and poetry that is timeless in its groove. She began her career as a full-time high school teacher, and much of her life since has been devoted to serving as a cultural worker and grassroots activist, using art and poetry to encourage dialogue and healing.

She has been a featured performer at many of the nation's premier spoken-word venues, including HBO's Def Poetry and BET's Lyric Cafe. You've seen and heard her work in commercials for BEATS by Dre products along with Serena Williams and she is the host for the inaugural season of The Golden Mic, brought to you by The Congo Network. She also had the privilege of speaking at the Panafest in Ghana, West Africa and has collaborated with artists and performers, including Hannibal Lokumbe (singing lead vocals for his score, "King and the Crescent City Moon"), Kalamu Ya Salaam, Sonia Sanchez, Wanda Coleman, Amiri Baraka, Mos Def, Eve Ensler, The Last Poets and many more.

For more info go to facebook.com/PoetSunniPatterson

www.ingramcontent.com/pod-product-compliance
Lightning Source LLC
Chambersburg PA
CBHW050704160426
43194CB00010B/1993